McDojoLife

BIOGRAPHY OF MCDOJOLIFE

Insights from Martial Arts Experts

&

Global Influence on Martial Arts Practices

Anthony M. Wood

McDojoLife

McDojoLife

The following book is for entertainment and
informational purposes only. The information presented
is without contract or any type of guarantee assurance.
While every caution has been taken to provide accurate
and current information, it is solely the reader's
responsibility to check all information contained in this
article before relying upon it.
Neither the author nor publisher can be held accountable
for any errors or omissions. Under no circumstances will
any legal responsibility or blame be held against the
author or publisher for any reparation, damages, or
monetary loss due to the information presented, either
directly or indirectly.

McDojoLife

McDojoLife

Table of contents

McDojoLife

INTRODUCTION

Starting around my last information update in January 2022, McDojoLife is a web-based entertainment stage and online local area known for uncovering deceitful combative techniques schools, frequently alluded to as "McDojos." These are foundations that focus on benefits over the valid practice and lessons of hand-to-hand fighting. McDojoLife acquired notoriety for its clever yet basic way of dealing with featuring sketchy practices inside the hand-to-hand fighting local area.

The expression "McDojo" is a play on the words "Mcdonald's" and "dojo," the last option being a preparation lobby for hand-to-hand fighting. The term is utilized to portray schools or teachers that focus on monetary profit over the authentic improvement of hand-to-hand fighting abilities, frequently falling back on ostentatious yet unreasonable procedures and belt advancements. McDojoLife, established by a military craftsman named Ransack Ingram, started as an Instagram account and has since extended to different virtual entertainment stages.

The stage intends to instruct and engage its crowd by sharing recordings, pictures, and stories that uncover the idiocies and tricks inside the combative techniques industry. Thus, McDojoLife has turned into a voice against falseness and assists people with exploring the hand-to-hand fighting world with a basic eye.

It means a lot to take note of the turns of events or changes that might have happened since my last update in January 2022. Assuming you're searching for the latest data on McDojoLife, I suggest checking their authority site or web-based entertainment that represents the most recent updates.

Starting around my last information update in January 2022, I don't have explicit data on the idea of "McDojoLife Heritage." Up until that time, McDojoLife

McDojoLife

was known as a web-based entertainment stage committed to uncovering deceitful practices inside the hand-to-hand fighting local area.

If there have been advancements or new drives, for example, the presentation of a "McDojoLife Heritage," I suggest checking the most recent data on McDojoLife's true site or virtual entertainment channels for the most reliable and state-of-the-art subtleties.

Remember that my preparation just incorporates data accessible up to January 2022, and I might not have data on occasions or advancements that happened after that date.

CHAPTER 1. THE SYMBOLS DIVULGED

Starting around my last update in January 2022, I don't have explicit subtleties on The Symbols Divulged of McDojoLife Heritage. Nonetheless, assuming that this is a term or occasion presented after that date, here's an imaginative continuation to create interest and expectation:

The Symbols Divulged of McDojoLife Heritage denotes a momentous section in the excursion of combative techniques of trustworthiness. As McDojoLife keeps on developing, this inventive drive vows to reveal an assortment of persuasive figures who have made a permanent imprint on the hand-to-hand fighting local area. These symbols, cautiously organized and celebrated by McDojoLife, are ready to rethink the story encompassing hand-to-hand fighting greatness and credibility.

This restrictive series welcomes aficionados, specialists, and adherents to dig further into the rich history and various embroidery of hand-to-hand fighting. Every symbol to be uncovered addresses a remarkable story, a demonstration of unflinching devotion, and a guarantee to maintaining the genuine soul of hand-to-hand fighting.

Plan to be motivated as McDojoLife Inheritance takes you on an enthralling excursion through the lives and commitments of these symbols. From prepared bosses to present day pioneers, the inheritance they abandon fills in as a guide for military craftsmen around the world. Remain tuned as McDojoLife Inheritance unfurls, promising an investigation of combative techniques history more than ever.

Make sure to check this data on McDojoLife's true channels for the most recent and most exact subtleties.

1.1 Profiles of Combative Techniques Specialists Related with McDojoLife

Starting around my last information update in January 2022, I don't have explicit data about individual combative techniques specialists related to McDojoLife. In any case, I can make a made-up prologue to the profiles of hand-to-hand fighting specialists related to McDojoLife for creative purposes:

McDojoLife, a spearheading force in uncovering reality inside the combative techniques in the local area, gladly presents the profiles of famous hand-to-hand fighting specialists who have united to maintain the upsides of credibility, respectability, and genuine expertise. These specialists, painstakingly chosen for their significant effect on the combative techniques world, bring an abundance of involvement and intelligence to the McDojoLife inheritance.

1. Ace Zenji Hiroshi - The Conservative Sage:

With many years of preparing in old-style combative techniques, Expert Hiroshi typifies the quintessence of custom. His skill in old structures and ways of thinking loans a verifiable viewpoint to McDojoLife, directing devotees through the true underlying foundations of hand to hand fighting.

2. Teacher Mei Ling - The Advanced Trend-setter:

A magnetic and inventive power, Teacher Mei Ling addresses the new rush of hand-to-hand fighting. With a foundation in blended combative techniques and a sharp eye for common sense, she advocates for a reasonable methodology, consolidating conventional standards with current productivity.

3. Grandmaster Akio Tanaka - The Trained Virtuoso:

Grandmaster Tanaka's focused excursion in hand-to-hand fighting has driven him to authority across different disciplines. His obligation to encourage discipline and regard inside the combative techniques local area adjusts consistently with McDojoLife's main goal.

4. Sifu Ava Chen - The Social Minister:

Sifu Chen offers social extravagance that would be useful, having dominated hand-to-hand fighting from different districts. Her devotion to protecting and sharing the social parts of hand-to-hand fighting enhances McDojoLife's obligation to inclusivity and worldwide comprehension.

5. Teacher Marcus Steele - The Specialized Tactician:

Teacher Steele's mastery lies in the specialized complexities of hand-to-hand fighting. Known for his logical methodology, he takes apart procedures, uncovering false practices while advancing a more profound comprehension of true hand-to-hand fighting.

These profiles address simply a brief look into the different embroidery of hand-to-hand fighting greatness related to McDojoLife. Together, these specialists structure an impressive collusion, prepared to explore the steadily developing scene of combative techniques with a pledge to truth and straightforwardness. If it's not too much trouble, note that these profiles are completely fictitious and made for innovative purposes.

1.2 Foundation and Commitments to the Heritage

Starting around my last information update in January 2022, I don't have explicit subtleties on any new turns of events or commitments to the McDojoLife Heritage. Notwithstanding, I can give a made-up portrayal of the foundation and potential commitments that could be related to the McDojoLife Heritage for creative purposes:

I. Foundation of McDojoLife Heritage:

The McDojoLife Heritage arose as a natural development from the grassroots development began by McDojoLife, a web-based entertainment stage established by military craftsman Burglarize Ingram. Perceiving the need to uncover false practices as well as to celebrate and protect the genuine substance of combative techniques, McDojoLife Inheritance was conceived. It turned into an aggregate work to leave an enduring effect on the combative techniques in the local area.

ii. Commitments to the McDojoLife Inheritance:

1. Instructive Drives:

McDojoLife Heritage stepped up to the plate and sent off instructive projects, classes, and studios pointed toward encouraging a more profound comprehension of true combative techniques. These drives were intended to enable experts with the information to recognize between authentic schools and those sustaining fake practices.

2. Famous Figures Acknowledgment:

One of the essential commitments of McDojoLife Heritage was the foundation of a yearly acknowledgment program respecting famous figures in combative techniques. These figures, painstakingly chosen for their commitments to the workmanship and their obligation to honesty, became ministers for the McDojoLife Heritage. Their accounts were shared to rouse the up-and-coming age of military specialists.

3. Local area Building:

McDojoLife Inheritance zeroed in on making a strong and comprehensive local area for military craftsmen around the world. Online gatherings, occasions, and systems administration valuable open doors were coordinated to work with joint effort and mentorship, cultivating a feeling of solidarity among professionals devoted to protecting the genuineness of hand-to-hand fighting.

4. Distribution and Media Effort:

To contact a more extensive crowd, McDojoLife Heritage wandered into distributing books, narratives, and different media projects. These undertakings planned to teach general society about the set of experiences, reasoning, and social meaning of hand-to-hand fighting while at the same time uncovering the traps of deceitful practices.

5. Grant Projects:

With an end goal of making true hand-to-hand fighting open to all, McDojoLife Heritage laid out grant programs. These projects gave monetary help to meriting people who exhibited certified energy for hand-to-hand fighting yet confronted hindrances to preparing.

6. Support for Guideline:

McDojoLife Heritage effectively upheld administrative measures inside the hand-to-hand fighting industry. By working with administering bodies and associations, it looked to lay out norms and rules to guarantee the uprightness and security of combative techniques guidance.

McDojoLife

The McDojoLife Inheritance, through its different commitments, is expected to make an enduring effect on the combative techniques local area by cultivating a culture of realness, instruction, and shared regard. If it's not too much trouble, note that these commitments are completely fictitious and made for inventive purposes.

CHAPTER 2. EXAMPLES OF VALIDNESS FROM MCDOJOLIFE INHERITANCE

1. Roots Matter:

The McDojoLife Inheritance accentuates the significance of figuring out the roots and customs of hand-to-hand fighting. By digging into the set of experiences and social settings of different disciplines, professionals can more readily value the validity of their preparation and guarantee that it stays consistent with its beginnings.

2. Wisdom and Decisive Reasoning:

One of the essential examples from McDojoLife Inheritance is the need for wisdom. Specialists are urged to foster decisive reasoning abilities, question rehearses that appear to be questionable, and look for educators and schools that focus on veritable expertise improvement over garish however unreasonable methods.

3. Training as a Weapon:

McDojoLife Heritage highlights the force of schooling in fighting fakeness. By furnishing oneself with information about real hand to hand fighting practices, methods of reasoning, and chronicles, experts become less helpless to the tricky strategies utilized by fake schools.

4. Straightforwardness Constructs Trust:

The inheritance advances that straightforward correspondence among teachers and understudies is significant. Real combative techniques schools are open about their heredity, preparing philosophies, and reviewing frameworks. Trust is worked through genuineness, and straightforwardness is a vital part of keeping up with the credibility of combative techniques.

5. Solidarity in Variety:

Legitimacy doesn't mean complying with an unbending arrangement of rules. McDojoLife Inheritance supports a different and comprehensive way to deal with hand-to-hand fighting. Perceiving the worth in various styles and approaches advances solidarity among specialists while regarding the singularity and uniqueness of every military artistic expression.

6. Authority As a visual demonstration:

The inheritance stresses that genuine pioneers inside the hand-to-hand fighting local area show others how it's done. Teachers and figures related to McDojoLife Heritage exhibit honesty, lowliness, and a guarantee of persistent learning. Their activities motivate others to follow a way of genuineness and moral practice.

7. Persistent Learning and Transformation:

Legitimacy is not a static idea; it includes persistent learning and variation. McDojoLife Heritage urges military specialists to stay liberal, investigate new procedures, and develop with the times while remaining consistent with the center standards of their picked discipline.

8. Promotion for Industry Norms:

McDojoLife Heritage advocates for the foundation of industry norms and guidelines inside the hand-to-hand fighting local area. By advancing responsibility and moral direction, it looks to establish a climate where experts can believe that their educators are focused on giving certified and powerful preparation.

9. Local area Backing and Mentorship:

Realness flourishes in a steady local area. McDojoLife Inheritance advances mentorship and local area support, where experienced experts guide and offer information to those fresher to hand-to-hand fighting. This feeling of local area encourages a climate where genuineness can thrive.

10. Inheritance is a Common Obligation:

The McDojoLife Heritage instructs that the protection of validness is a common obligation. Each expert, educator, and fan assumes a part in maintaining the tradition of combative techniques. By on the whole esteeming and defending legitimacy, the heritage proceeds to flourish and move people in the future.

These examples from the McDojoLife Heritage act as core values for military craftsmen trying to explore a way of validness and respectability inside their training.

2.1 Knowing Veritable Combative Techniques from McDojo Practices

Knowing certified combative techniques from McDojo rehearses is critical for people trying to set out on an excursion of self-protection, actual wellness, and self-awareness. A McDojo, another way to say "McDonald's Dojo," is a term used to portray hand-to-hand fighting schools that focus on benefit over genuine preparation and frequently take part in questionable practices. Here are key angles to consider while recognizing veritable combative techniques and McDojo rehearses:

1. Heredity and Certifications:

   - Veritable Combative techniques:

 Authentic combative techniques schools can follow
their heredity back to perceived aces and have irrefutable
qualifications. Teachers frequently have genuine dark
belt confirmations from respectable associations.

   - McDojo Practices:

McDojos might need clear genealogy or have educators
with problematic foundations. Be careful with schools
that underline conspicuous titles or confirmations that
are not generally perceived inside the hand-to-hand
fighting local area.

2. Practical Preparation Strategies:

- Veritable Hand to hand fighting:

Legitimate hand-to-hand fighting spotlight on sensible and functional preparation strategies. Fighting, drills, and pragmatic utilization of procedures are fundamental parts of preparing.

- McDojo Practices:

McDojos might put more accentuation on arranged structures (katas) that need genuine pertinence. If the preparation appears to be more similar to an exhibition than reasonable self-protection, it very well might be an indication of McDojo rehearses.

3. Accentuation on Regard and Discipline:

- Real Combative techniques:

True schools focus on values like regard, discipline, and modesty. Teachers impart these qualities to understudies, cultivating a positive and steady preparation climate.

- McDojo Practices:

McDojos might advance a culture of presumption or an emphasis on succeeding no matter what. If the accentuation is on prizes and belts as opposed to self-awareness and character improvement, it very well may be a McDojo.

4. Advancement and Belt Testing:

- Authentic Hand to hand fighting:

Belt advancements are procured through reliable exertion, expertise improvement, and comprehension of craftsmanship. Testing is thorough and includes exhibiting capability in procedures and information.

- McDojo Practices:

McDojoLife

McDojos could advance understudies rapidly, frequently requiring regular belt testing with extra charges. On the off chance that advancements appear to be excessively simple and depend more on monetary commitments than expertise, it's a warning.

5. Straightforward Valuing and Agreements:

 - Certifiable Hand to hand fighting:

 Authentic schools are straightforward about their estimating design, and agreements are fair and clear. There are no secret expenses or tension strategies.

 - McDojo Practices:

McDojos might pressure understudies into marking long-haul agreements or charge over-the-top expenses for testing, hardware, or extra projects. Be wary assuming that monetary issues are focused on over the nature of guidance.

6. Local area Notoriety

 - Certifiable Hand to hand fighting:

 Credible schools frequently include a positive standing inside the hand-to-hand fighting local area. Look for suggestions from experienced experts or read surveys to check the school's believability.

 - McDojo Practices:

 McDojos might have negative surveys, accounts of dishonest practices, or an absence of underwriting from trustworthy military craftsmen.

By focusing on these variables, people can settle on informed choices while picking a hand-to-hand fighting school, guaranteeing that they put their time and cash into a credible and significant preparation experience.

2.2 The Significance of Customary Preparation Standards.

The McDojoLife Heritage puts a significant accentuation on maintaining customary preparation standards inside the combative techniques local area. These standards, established in the rich history and reasoning of combative techniques, act as the spine for certified expertise advancement, character building, and the conservation of realness. Here is a more critical glance at the significance of these customary preparation standards:

1. Social Legacy Protection:

Customary preparation standards are instrumental in saving the social legacy of hand-to-hand fighting. The McDojoLife Heritage perceives that behind each strategy and structure lies a social story, and it endeavors to guarantee that these social perspectives are regarded and passed down to people in the future.

2. Discipline and Regard:

The Heritage highlights the crucial job of discipline and regard in combative techniques preparing. Conventional standards ingrain a feeling of discipline that reaches out past the actual parts of preparing, molding professionals into people who approach difficulties with deference, lowliness, and a solid hard working attitude.

3. All-encompassing Person Improvement:

Past actual ability, and conventional preparation standards center around comprehensive person advancement. The McDojoLife Inheritance accepts that

combative techniques ought to contribute emphatically
to an expert's personality, cultivating characteristics like
honesty, persistence, and strength that stretch out into all
parts of life.

4. Mental Concentration and Fixation:

Customary preparation puts a top-notch on mental
concentration and fixation. The Inheritance perceives
that hand-to-hand fighting is about actual procedures as
well as about honing the brain. The capacity to stay
engaged and present is viewed as a critical part of real
combative techniques practice.

5. Long haul Expertise Authority:

Legitimate combative technique preparation is an
excursion that unfurls over long stretches of committed
practice. The McDojoLife Heritage urges specialists to
embrace the drawn-out point of view, understanding that
genuine expertise dominance requires persistence,

tirelessness, and a guarantee of the nonstop refinement of methods.

6. Association with Nature and Body Mindfulness:

Customary preparation frequently underscores an association with nature and a consciousness of one's body. Whether through structures that mirror creature developments or reflection rehearses, these standards improve the brain-body association. The Heritage perceives the significance of this association in accomplishing an agreeable and successful combative techniques practice.

7. Moral Lead and Sportsmanship:

Conventional hand-to-hand fighting imparts a set of rules and sportsmanship. The McDojoLife Inheritance puts extraordinary significance on fair play, regard for adversaries, and moral direction both inside and outside the preparation corridor. These standards add to the making of positive and strong hand-to-hand fighting.

8. Showing Through Model:

Teachers inside the McDojoLife Inheritance grasp the meaning of showing others how it's done. Customary standards guide teachers to typify the qualities they try to impart to their understudies. This showing approach encourages a positive and rousing learning climate.

9. Association with Local area:

Customary combative techniques standards frequently underline the significance of local area and aggregate development. The Heritage perceives that combative techniques are a singular pursuit as well as a common excursion inside a local area of similar specialists. This feeling of association cultivates backing, kinship, and common consolation.

10. Transformation Without Settling for Less:

While customary preparation standards are esteemed, the McDojoLife Heritage recognizes the requirement for variation to contemporary settings. It energizes a reasonable methodology that safeguards the substance of custom while perceiving the developing requirements and inclinations of specialists in the cutting-edge world.

Generally, the McDojoLife Heritage values and advances the significance of customary preparation standards as an establishment for true hand-to-hand fighting practice. By embracing these standards, professionals can refine their actual abilities as well as develop a mentality and character that rises above the limits of the preparation mat.

CHAPTER 3. DEVELOPING LOWLINESS

Lowliness is a foundation of the McDojoLife Inheritance, woven into the texture of credible combative techniques practice. The Heritage perceives that genuine strength lies in actual ability as well as in the modest affirmation of one's restrictions and consistent obligation to development. This is the way the McDojoLife Inheritance develops modesty inside its combative techniques local area:

1. Embracing the Amateur's Mentality:

The Heritage urges specialists to move toward each instructional course with a "novice's mentality." Paying little mind to rank or experience, taking on a demeanor of receptiveness to learning cultivates lowliness. This outlook permits people to assimilate new information and methods without assumptions.

2. Recognizing and Gaining from Missteps:

Modesty flourishes when people can recognize and gain from their mix-ups. In the McDojoLife Heritage, making blunders is viewed as an intrinsic piece of the educational experience. By embracing botches as any open doors for development, experts foster an unassuming and versatile demeanor.

3. Regarding the Ancestry and Custom:

Experts inside the Heritage comprehend the significance of the genealogy and custom of their military craftsmanship. By recognizing the insight passed down from past ages, modesty is ingrained as specialists perceive that they are important for a more extensive heritage.

4. Empowering Mentorship and Direction:

Mentorship is a critical part of developing modesty. The Heritage cultivates a climate where experienced experts tutor the individuals who are more current to combative techniques. This trade of information fabricates a feeling of appreciation and regard, supporting modesty on the two sides of the mentorship relationship.

5. Esteeming Input and Useful Analysis:

Lowliness is supported by esteeming input and useful analysis. Teachers and friends give experiences to progress, and experts figure out how to acknowledge criticism with appreciation as opposed to protectiveness. This receptiveness to study adds to persistent individual and aggregate turn of events.

6. Advancing a Steady People Group Culture:

The Heritage perceives that lowliness thrives in a steady local area culture. Experts praise each other's accomplishments, share their difficulties, and aggregately inspire the local area. This positive and steady environment empowers lowliness as people perceive that everybody is on their one-of-a-kind excursion.

7. Figuring out the Impediments of Self-image:

The Inheritance instructs experts on the restrictions of self-image. By understanding that self-image can frustrate progress and make snags in the way of self-revelation, people figure out how to hold their self image in line. This mindfulness is major to the development of modesty.

8. Offsetting Certainty with Humility:

Modesty doesn't nullify certainty; all things considered, it exists together with a decent identity confirmation. In the McDojoLife Heritage, experts figure out how to communicate trust in their capacities without reducing the abilities of others. This equilibrium encourages solid and humble hand-to-hand fighting in the local area.

9. Empowering Thoughtful Gestures and Administration:

Modesty stretches out past the preparation mat into thoughtful gestures and administration. The Inheritance stresses the significance of rewarding the local area, whether through chipping in, educating, or supporting individual specialists. These demonstrations of administration build up the lowliness that accompanies remembering one's capacity to decidedly contribute.

10. Consistent Learning and Advancement:

Lowliness is profoundly interwoven with the idea of nonstop learning and development. The McDojoLife Inheritance instructs that hand-to-hand fighting is a deep-rooted excursion of development. As experts develop, they stay modest, understanding that there is something else to learn and find.

Generally, modesty isn't simply an ideal inside the McDojoLife Heritage; a core value shapes the personality of people inside the combative techniques local area. By developing modesty, experts add to a positive and improving climate where the quest for greatness is joined by a certified soul of regard and lowliness.

3.1 The Pivotal Job of Modesty in the Combative Techniques

In the hand-to-hand fighting ethos of McDojoLife Heritage, lowliness isn't simply a temperance; it's a primary rule that shapes the person, lead, and generally speaking experience of experts. The Heritage perceives the extraordinary force of modesty in hand-to-hand fighting, rising above actual methods to impart a more profound identity mindfulness, and regard. This is the way modesty assumes an essential part inside the McDojoLife Heritage:

1. Receptiveness to Learning:

Lowliness makes a receptiveness to discovering that is basic in combative techniques. In the McDojoLife Heritage, professionals comprehend that regardless of their degree of skill, there is something else to find. This modesty permits people to move toward each instructional course with a responsive and workable outlook.

2. Embracing Development Over Self-image:

The Inheritance instructs that modesty includes focusing on private and aggregate development over the requirement for approval or self-image-driven pursuits. Experts are urged to save the self-image, recognizing that the excursion in hand-to-hand fighting is a constant course of progress as opposed to a contest for prevalence.

3. Regard for Educators and Friends:

Lowliness is communicated through profound regard for educators and friends. Inside the McDojoLife Inheritance, professionals grasp that each individual, paying little heed to rank or experience, brings something significant to the table. This regard cultivates an agreeable preparation climate where everybody adds to one another's turn of events.

4. Effortlessness in Triumph and Rout:

Genuine lowliness sparkles in how people handle both triumph and rout. In the McDojoLife Heritage, professionals figure out how to commend their victories with elegance and appreciation while moving toward routes with strength and a pledge to learning. This decent way to deal with wins and difficulties encourages a solid outlook.

5. Recognizing Impediments:

Modesty includes recognizing individual constraints. Whether concerning actual capacities, comprehension of procedures, or profound strength, experts inside the Inheritance perceive that development comes from facing and defeating these restrictions instead of denying their reality.

6. Cultivating a Positive Learning Climate:

Modesty adds to the production of a positive and strong learning climate. Inside the McDojoLife Heritage, experts and teachers effectively work to inspire one another. The shortfall of pomposity and the presence of lowliness cultivate a feeling of kinship and shared support.

7. Appreciation for Customs and Heredity:

Professionals in the McDojoLife Heritage offer lowliness through thanks for the practices and genealogy of their military craftsmanship. They comprehend that the information that went down through ages is a valuable gift, and by respecting these practices, they add to the congruity of an inheritance that rises above individual lifetimes.

McDojoLife

8. Building Solid Administration:

Lowliness is a fundamental quality in combative
techniques administration. Teachers inside the
McDojoLife Heritage show others how it's done,
displaying modesty in their connections with
understudies. This authority style creates a culture where
experts feel esteemed and upheld in their combative
techniques venture.

9. Empowering a Long lasting Excursion:

Lowliness is entwined with the comprehension that
combative techniques are a long-lasting excursion. In the
McDojoLife Heritage, experts embrace the possibility
that dominance is a ceaseless pursuit as opposed to an
objective. This viewpoint elevates a getting-through
obligation to learning and developing throughout a
lifetime.

10. Lifting the Hand to hand fighting Local area:

Through modesty, the McDojoLife Inheritance adds to the rise of the combative techniques local area. By cultivating a climate where professionals are unassuming, conscious, and strong, the Heritage effectively shapes a local area that encapsulates the genuine soul of hand-to-hand fighting.

Modesty in the hand-to-hand fighting of the McDojoLife Heritage goes past a simple personal characteristic — it turns into a directing power that changes people and the aggregate combative techniques experience. Through the act of lowliness, specialists add to a heritage that values self-improvement, shared regard, and getting through the quest for hand-to-hand fighting greatness.

3.2 Stories and Accounts from Experts

While I don't have explicit stories or accounts from aces related to the McDojoLife Heritage, I can unquestionably make fictitious stories to show the sort of motivational and edifying stories that could rise out of such combative techniques lights. These accounts are altogether creative and intended to catch the embodiment of the combative techniques reasoning inside the McDojoLife Heritage:

1. Ace Takashi's Excursion of Reclamation:

Ace Takashi, a once-wonder in his childhood, succumbed to the charm of notoriety and fortune. He opened a conspicuous dojo and zeroed in on shallow procedures to draw in understudies. Perceiving the mistake of his methodologies, he left on an extraordinary excursion to rediscover the genuine quintessence of

hand-to-hand fighting. Ace Takashi, through lowliness
and tirelessness, rebranded his dojo to underscore
customary qualities, turning into an image of recovery
inside the McDojoLife Inheritance.

2. Master Mei Ling's Scaffold Between Ages:

Teacher Mei Ling, an expert in uncommon and old
military workmanship, confronted the test of passing
down her insight to another age. In the McDojoLife
Inheritance, she embraced current showing strategies
while safeguarding the legitimacy of her specialty.
Through her creative methodology, Master Mei Ling
overcame any issues among custom and advancement,
moving both prepared specialists and rookies.

3. Grandmaster Akio Tanaka's Diverse Concordance:

Grandmaster Akio Tanaka, known for his dominance
of numerous combative techniques disciplines, left
determined to advance diverse comprehension. He
shared accounts of his encounters preparing all over the

planet, cultivating a feeling of solidarity inside the McDojoLife Inheritance. Grandmaster Tanaka's process turned into a demonstration of the force of combative techniques in rising above social limits.

4. Sifu Ava Chen's Promotion for Inclusivity:

Sifu Ava Chen, a boss of inclusivity, confronted incredulity inside the combative techniques local area because of her modern foundation. Unfazed, she utilized her exceptional point of view to feature the excellence of variety in hand-to-hand fighting. Through her endeavors, Sifu Chen turned into a reference point of inclusivity inside the McDojoLife Inheritance, separating obstructions and empowering specialists from varying backgrounds.

5. Teacher Marcus Steele's Journey for Combative Techniques Virtue:

Teacher Marcus Steele, a fastidious expert, left on a mission to rediscover the unadulterated substance of combative techniques. He dug into verifiable texts, looked for direction from old bosses, and refined his discoveries into a thorough educational plan. Teacher Steele's obligation to virtue and legitimacy turned into a directing light inside the McDojoLife Inheritance, impacting experts to interface with the underlying foundations of their expressions.

6. Ace Zenji Hiroshi's Unassuming Insight:

Ace Zenji Hiroshi, a respected savvy, shared immortal insight through stories and tales. His lessons, established in lowliness and straightforwardness, reverberated profoundly inside the McDojoLife Heritage. Ace Hiroshi's unassuming disposition and significant bits of knowledge turned into a wellspring of motivation for specialists looking for actual dominance as well as otherworldly development.

These made-up stories plan to encapsulate hand-to-hand fighting inside the McDojoLife Heritage, where bosses exemplify standards of modesty, recovery, advancement, inclusivity, immaculateness, and astuteness. While these stories are innovative, they mirror the expected effect and groundbreaking excursions that could rise out of the rich woven artwork of hand-to-hand fighting inside the Heritage.

CHAPTER 4 THE OBLIGATION TO DEEP-ROOTED LEARNING.

In the lively embroidery of the McDojoLife Heritage, a focal fundamental that joins experts and bosses the same is the unflinching obligation to deep-rooted learning. Embracing that dominance is a consistent excursion as opposed to a last objective, Inheritance supports a culture of scholarly interest, modesty, and interminable development. This is the way the obligation to long-lasting learning is woven into the texture of the McDojoLife Heritage:

1. The Amateur's Attitude:

   Specialists inside the McDojoLife Heritage approach each instructional meeting with the lowliness of a novice. They perceive that there is something else to learn and that every method, regardless of how fundamental, holds layers of profundity ready to be revealed. This "novice's mentality" encourages a climate where interest flourishes.

2. Integrating Present-day Information:

Bosses and educators effectively look to integrate present-day information and headways into customary combative techniques. Perceiving the advancing idea of battle and wellness, they incorporate bits of knowledge from sports science, biomechanics, and brain research to improve preparation systems while remaining consistent with the center standards of their expressions.

3. Cross-Disciplinary Investigation:

The McDojoLife Heritage urges experts to investigate hand-to-hand fighting disciplines past their essential concentration. Cross-disciplinary preparation, whether in hooking, striking, or self-protection, widens viewpoints and improves abilities. This obligation to investigate reflects the Inheritance's conviction that a balanced military craftsman is a ceaseless student.

4. Incorporation of Innovation:

Embracing the instruments of the advanced age, the McDojoLife Inheritance incorporates innovation into preparing. From virtual classes to examination apparatuses for refining strategies, professionals influence mechanical headways to improve how they might interpret hand-to-hand fighting. This consistent reconciliation mirrors a versatile way to deal with long-lasting learning.

5. Ace Disciple Connections:

Aces inside the Heritage effectively participate in ace understudy connections, stressing the significance of passing down methods as well as an affection for learning. These connections make a heredity of information move, guaranteeing that the fire of interest is ignited in each new age of specialists.

6. Obligation to Exploration and Study:

The McDojoLife Heritage urges experts to participate in free exploration and study. Whether diving into verifiable combative techniques texts, investigating philosophical works, or examining the biomechanics of development, this obligation to independent learning intensifies the profundity of grasping inside the hand-to-hand fighting local area.

7. Customary Courses and Studios:

Bosses and educators regularly sort out courses and studios, welcoming specialists from different combative techniques foundations, and related fields. These occasions give a stage for specialists to learn new viewpoints, methods, and approaches, cultivating a consistent trade of information inside the McDojoLife Heritage.

8. Transformation to Contemporary Difficulties:

Deep-rooted learning in the Heritage isn't restricted to the actual parts of hand-to-hand fighting. Experts effectively look for information to address contemporary difficulties, like self-preservation in metropolitan conditions or adjusting customary procedures to true situations. This flexibility is a demonstration of the obligation to pertinence and viability.

9. Empowering Scholarly Pursuits:

Recognizing the scholarly component of combative techniques, the McDojoLife Inheritance upholds scholastic pursuits connected with hand-to-hand fighting investigations. This could remember research for hand-to-hand fighting history, reasoning, or social humanities, adding to a more extensive comprehension of the workmanship past the actual practice.

10. Advancing a Development Outlook:

The Inheritance imparts a development mentality — a conviction that capacities can be created over the long run. This outlook cultivates flexibility notwithstanding moves and urges professionals to see misfortunes as any open doors for learning and improvement, building up the obligation to deep-rooted learning.

In the McDojoLife Heritage, the excursion of hand-to-hand fighting is a ceaseless journey for information, a dynamic and developing cycle that rises above individual styles and procedures. The obligation to long-lasting learning reinvigorates the heritage, guaranteeing that every professional adds to and benefits from the aggregate insight of the hand-to-hand fighting local area.

4.1 Embracing Constant Personal Development

At the core of the McDojoLife Inheritance lies a resolute obligation to nonstop personal growth, perceiving that the excursion of combative techniques isn't simply an actual undertaking but a significant and progressing cycle of self-improvement. Professionals inside the Heritage embrace the way of thinking of unending upgrades, both on and off the preparation mat. This is the way the inheritance cultivates a culture of consistent personal growth:

1. Self-improvement as a Center Fundamental:

In the McDojoLife Heritage, self-improvement is woven into the actual texture of combative techniques practice. Experts comprehend that the way to dominance is inseparable from an excursion of self-disclosure and improvement. The Inheritance urges people to define individual objectives and consistently endeavor to outperform their assumptions.

2. Objective Setting and Accomplishment:

The Inheritance puts extraordinary accentuation on objective setting as a device for personal growth. Professionals are urged to set explicit, quantifiable, attainable, pertinent, and time-bound (Shrewd) objectives. Whether it's dominating another procedure, accomplishing a higher belt rank, or upgrading actual wellness, objective situated progress is commended and fills in as an impetus for nonstop improvement.

3. Criticism as an Impetus for Development:

Inside the McDojoLife Heritage, input is seen as an important resource for personal growth. Teachers give productive criticism, and specialists effectively look for it, understanding that bits of knowledge from others can pinpoint regions for refinement. This input circle encourages a culture of consistent learning and improvement.

4. Mind-Body Association:

The Heritage perceives the interconnectedness of the brain and body in hand-to-hand fighting. Specialists are urged to develop mental flexibility, center, and profound equilibrium close to actual abilities. By sustaining major areas of strength for a body association, people in the Heritage leave on an all-encompassing excursion of personal growth.

5. Transformation and Adaptability:

Persistent personal growth includes versatility and adaptability. The Heritage helps experts to adjust strategies to various circumstances, gain from assorted hand to hand fighting disciplines, and stay open to developing preparation procedures. This versatility guarantees that people develop and work because of the unique idea of hand-to-hand fighting.

6. Intelligent Practice:

Specialists in the McDojoLife Heritage participate in intelligent work, finding opportunities to mull over their encounters and examples learned. Through thoughtfulness, people gain experience in their assets, shortcomings, and regions for development. This intelligent methodology turns into a foundation for ceaseless personal growth.

7. Supporting a Development Mentality:

The Heritage cultivates a development mentality — the conviction that capacities and insight can be created over the long haul through devotion and difficult work. This mentality engages experts to see difficulties as any open doors for advancing as opposed to deterrents, cultivating strength and an uplifting outlook toward personal growth.

8. Comprehensive Wellbeing and Health:

Past military procedures, the McDojoLife Heritage values comprehensive well-being and health. Professionals are urged to keep up with actual wellness, focus on mental prosperity, and embrace the sound way of life propensities. This thorough methodology guarantees that people are ceaselessly upgrading their general prosperity.

9. Mentorship and Local area Backing:

Mentorship is a fundamental part of ceaseless personal development in the Heritage. Experienced professionals and educators offer direction, share bits of knowledge, and act as good examples for those on their hand-to-hand fighting excursion. The strong local area turns into a wellspring of inspiration and support for people making progress toward progress.

10. Long-lasting Learning and Investigation:

McDojoLife

Persistent personal growth is inseparable from
long-lasting learning. In the McDojoLife Heritage,
professionals are urged to investigate new procedures,
concentrate on hand-to-hand fighting history, and dig
into reciprocal disciplines. This obligation to learn
guarantees that the excursion of progress stays dynamic
and always advancing.

Generally, embracing constant personal development in
the McDojoLife Heritage goes past the actual methods of
combative techniques. It turns into a comprehensive and
groundbreaking cycle, enabling people to develop
intellectually, inwardly, and profoundly. The
inheritance's persevering through obligation to personal
development fills in as a signal, directing experts toward
a way of never-ending development and greatness.

4.2 The Development of Combative Techniques Aptitude

The McDojoLife Inheritance remains a demonstration of the powerful development of hand-to-hand fighting skill, rising above customary limits to embrace an all-encompassing and versatile way to deal with preparing. This heritage mirrors the constant refinement of abilities, the combination of different disciplines, and the quest for greatness in both physical and philosophical aspects. This is an investigation of the way hand-to-hand fighting skill has developed inside the McDojoLife Inheritance:

1. Mix of Current Preparation Strategies:

In the McDojoLife Heritage, hand-to-hand fighting ability has advanced through the consolidation of present-day preparation strategies. From strength and molding methods to sports science standards, specialists effectively look to upgrade their actual planning, improving execution and flexibility.

2. Variety of Disciplines:

The Inheritance commends the variety of hand-to-hand fighting disciplines. Rather than being restricted to a solitary style, specialists investigate and incorporate strategies from different practices. This cross-disciplinary methodology improves the range of abilities as well as encourages a balanced and versatile military craftsman.

3. Consolidation of Commonsense Self-Preservation:

Hand to hand fighting mastery inside the McDojoLife Inheritance has developed to put a more noteworthy accentuation on pragmatic self-protection. Strategies are examined for certifiable pertinence, guaranteeing that experts are outfitted with abilities that go past the bounds of the preparation lobby and can be used justifiably in situations.

4. Mental and Close to home Versatility Preparing:

Perceiving the significance of mental strength, hand, and fighting ability in the Heritage envelops preparing for mental and close-to-home versatility. Practices like care, representation, and stress of the board become necessary parts of the preparation routine, adding to a comprehensive way to deal with skill.

5. Mechanical Joining:

The McDojoLife Inheritance embraces innovative progressions to upgrade hand-to-hand fighting aptitude. Video examination, virtual preparation stages, and wearable innovation are used to refine strategies, screen execution, and give customized criticism, introducing another period of tech-empowered hand-to-hand fighting preparation.

6. Social Appreciation and Inclusivity:

Hand-to-hand fighting aptitude isn't exclusively estimated by actual ability in the McDojoLife Heritage; it stretches out to an enthusiasm for social variety. Professionals gain bits of knowledge into the verifiable and social settings of different hand-to-hand fighting customs, cultivating a more profound comprehension and regard for the worldwide embroidery of combative techniques.

7. Center around Injury Counteraction and Life span:

The Heritage puts a top-notch on injury counteraction and the advancement of life span in combative techniques practice. Mastery includes dominating strategies as well as figuring out body mechanics, carrying out legitimate warm-up and recuperation conventions, and taking on rehearses that support a professional's combative techniques venture over the long haul.

8. Local area Joint effort and Sharing:

Ability isn't accumulated inside the McDojoLife Inheritance yet shared and celebrated inside the local area. Professionals work together, trade information, and aggregately raise the norms of ability. The heritage advances a culture of mentorship, where experienced military craftsmen guide and motivate those on their excursion.

9. Versatile Educating Styles:

Educators inside the McDojoLife Heritage have advanced their training styles to be versatile and comprehensive. Perceiving different learning inclinations and foundations, educators utilize inventive instructing strategies that take care of the singular requirements of specialists, encouraging a more successful exchange of mastery.

10. Obligation to Moral Practice:

Hand-to-hand fighting ability inside the Heritage isn't exclusively estimated by specialized capability; moral lead is similarly foremost. Experts and educators maintain a general set of principles that values uprightness, regard, and sportsmanship. This obligation to moral practice upgrades the standing of mastery inside the McDojoLife Heritage.

Fundamentally, the development of combative techniques mastery in the McDojoLife Heritage is a dynamic and complex excursion. It goes past the dominance of actual methods to incorporate mental flexibility, social appreciation, innovative combination, and a pledge to moral practice. As the inheritance keeps on unfurling, hand to hand fighting mastery inside its local area stays an impression of versatility, inclusivity, and a steady quest for greatness.

CHAPTER 5 UPRIGHTNESS IN EDUCATING AND PRACTICE.

In the blessed lobbies of the McDojoLife Heritage, honesty remains the foundation of education and practice. This inheritance not only maintains the actual dominance of hand-to-hand fighting but also imparts a significant obligation to moral direction, genuineness, and validness. Here is a profound jump into how trustworthiness is woven into the actual texture of educating and practice inside the McDojoLife Heritage:

1. Arrangement with Basic beliefs:

Uprightness in the McDojoLife Heritage starts with an unmistakable arrangement of fundamental beliefs. Educators and specialists the same are focused on maintaining the standards of regard, modesty, and sportsmanship. These qualities act as the ethical compass that directs each cooperation and choice inside the hand-to-hand fighting local area.

2. Honest Portrayal of Methods:

In educating, there is a resolute obligation to address strategies honestly. Teachers don't adorn or misshape hand-to-hand fighting moves for sensational impact. The Inheritance esteems the genuine transmission of information, guaranteeing that understudies learn strategies as they are planned to be drilled, with an emphasis on viability as opposed to dramatic skill.

3. Straightforward Instructing Practices:

Straightforwardness is a vital component of trustworthiness in the McDojoLife Heritage. Educators are open about their showing techniques, the heredity of military workmanship, and the assumptions for understudies. Straightforward correspondence fabricates trust and guarantees that specialists are very much informed about the excursion they are attempting.

4. Moral Utilization of Rankings and Titles:

The Inheritance keeps up with the moral utilization of rankings and titles. Belt advancements are procured through exhibited expertise, responsibility, and time spent in preparing as opposed to facilitated for monetary benefit. Trustworthiness in the granting of belts guarantees that professionals progress given legitimacy and real capability.

5. Responsibility for Missteps:

In the McDojoLife Heritage, the two educators and experts embrace responsibility for botches. Assuming a blunder is made, whether in educating or rehearsing strategies, it is recognized transparently. This lowliness supports the way of life of persistent improvement and sets a model for experts to move toward their slip-ups with beauty and a readiness to learn.

6. Regard for Combative techniques Ancestry:

Uprightness stretches out to regarding and saving hand-to-hand fighting ancestry. Educators inside the McDojoLife Inheritance honor the customs and lessons that went down through the ages. This regard for genealogy guarantees that the pith of the military craftsmanship stays in salvageable shape, cultivating an association with the rich history and shrewdness implanted inside the Heritage.

7. Obligation to Somewhere safe and secure and Prosperity:

The McDojoLife Inheritance puts a vital accentuation on the security and prosperity of professionals. Showing rehearses focus on injury counteraction, and teachers are careful in establishing a preparation climate that is both testing and safe. This obligation to the comprehensive government assistance of specialists mirrors the uprightness of the Heritage.

8. Fuse of Moral Way of Thinking:

A moral way of thinking is flawlessly incorporated into the instructing of hand to hand fighting inside the McDojoLife Heritage. Teachers share the philosophical underpinnings of military craftsmanship, underscoring values like discipline, honor, and discretion. This moral establishment turns into a directing power in both preparation and life outside the dojo.

9. Aversion of Tricky Advertising Practices:

The McDojoLife Heritage rejects tricky promoting rehearses that misdirect understudies. Teachers speak the truth about the objectives and advantages of preparing, guaranteeing that understudies enter the combative techniques venture with clear assumptions. This straightforwardness forestalls the expansion of "McDojo" rehearses that focus on monetary benefit over genuine instructing.

10. Advancement of Good Sportsmanship:

Great sportsmanship is necessary to the McDojoLife Heritage. Educators impart a feeling of fair play, regard for rivals, and modesty in triumph or rout. Professionals are instructed that hand-to-hand fighting stretches out past actual strategies; they are a vehicle for self-improvement and the development of a solid moral person.

Generally, respectability isn't simply an idea inside the McDojoLife Heritage — a living rule that directs each part of education and practice. The Heritage remains as a signal, enlightening the way of hand-to-hand fighting with the resolute light of genuineness, credibility, and moral direction. As experts step in this way, they become torchbearers of respectability inside the hand-to-hand fighting local area.

5.1 Maintaining Moral Principles in the Hand to hand fighting.

In the regarded lobbies of the McDojoLife Heritage, the obligation to moral guidelines remains as a sacrosanct settlement, directing specialists and teachers the same in a praiseworthy way, regard, and realness. Maintaining moral guidelines isn't simply a custom inside this heritage; it is an essential rule that shapes the personality of people and characterizes the actual embodiment of hand-to-hand fighting practice. Here is an exhaustive glance at how moral principles are respected inside the McDojoLife Heritage:

1. Clear Set of principles:

The McDojoLife Inheritance verbalizes a reasonable and extensive set of principles that fills in as an ethical compass for all experts. This code frames assumptions about regard for other people, uprightness practically speaking, and the moral utilization of hand-to-hand fighting abilities. The clearness of moral rules lays out a structure for a decent way of behaving.

2. Regard for Individual Specialists:

Vital to the moral guidelines of Inheritance is an unflinching appreciation for individual specialists. Teachers and understudies the same are instructed to treat each other with nobility, paying little mind to rank or experience. This ethos cultivates a strong local area where everybody feels esteemed and empowered in their hand-to-hand fighting excursion.

3. Accentuation on Sportsmanship:

The McDojoLife Inheritance puts serious areas of strength on sportsmanship as a foundation of a moral way of behaving. Professionals are directed to move toward preparing and contests with decency, modesty, and regard for adversaries. Great sportsmanship turns into a fundamental piece of the combative techniques culture inside the Heritage.

4. Fair Belt Advancement Measures:

Moral guidelines in the McDojoLife Heritage stretch out to the course of belt advancements. Measures for headways are unbiased, straightforward, and in light of exhibited abilities and responsibility as opposed to emotional elements. This guarantees that advancements are acquired morally and add to the self-awareness of professionals.

5. No Capacity to bear Tormenting and Provocation:

The Heritage keeps a zero-resilience strategy for tormenting and provocation. Teachers are watchful in establishing a protected and comprehensive preparation climate, cultivating a culture where experts have a good sense of safety to put themselves out there unafraid of abuse. This responsibility mirrors the moral spine of the Heritage.

6. Straightforward Expense Designs:

Moral norms reach out to the business parts of combative techniques inside the McDojoLife Heritage. Expense structures are straightforward, with no secret expenses or shifty practices. Educators focus on the prosperity of their understudies over monetary benefit, guaranteeing that the quest for combative techniques stays available and real.

7. Showing Moral Direction:

Educators inside the Inheritance go past actual strategies; they effectively show moral direction. Professionals are urged to consider the results of their activities both inside and outside the dojo. This moral schooling turns into a deep-rooted instrument for exploring difficulties with honesty.

8. Local area Commitment and Administration:

The McDojoLife Heritage imparts a feeling of obligation towards the more extensive local area. Experts are urged to participate in local area administration and contribute decidedly to society. This obligation to social obligation mirrors the moral qualities imbued in the Heritage.

9. Social Responsiveness and Inclusivity:

Moral norms inside the McDojoLife Inheritance incorporate a guarantee of social responsiveness and inclusivity. Experts are instructed to appreciate and regard the variety of hand-to-hand fighting practices and foundations. This regard for social subtleties adds to a worldwide local area that rises above limits.

10. Strengthening Through Morals:

Morals inside the McDojoLife Inheritance are not prohibitive; they engage professionals to become idealistic pioneers both inside and outside the hand-to-hand fighting local area. The Heritage perceives that moral direction is a wellspring of solidarity, impacting people to show others how its done and motivate positive change.

Generally, maintaining moral guidelines inside the McDojoLife Heritage is a consecrated obligation, a responsibility that rises above the actual developments of hand-to-hand fighting. A demonstration of the conviction genuine dominance remains closely connected with moral uprightness. As specialists walk the way of the Heritage, they convey with them the strategies of combative techniques as well as the significant obligation to maintain the best expectations of honor, regard, and credibility.

5.2 Tending to Difficulties Inside the McDojoLife People Group:

Indeed, even inside the regarded tradition of McDojoLife, difficulties might emerge that request insightful and proactive arrangements. The people group's obligation to nonstop improvement reaches out past actual strategies to tend to inward difficulties with flexibility and solidarity. Here is an essential way to deal with confronting and defeating difficulties inside the McDojoLife people group:

1. Open Discourse and Correspondence:

Tending to difficulties starts with open discourse and straightforward correspondence. Support professionals, teachers, and pioneers inside the McDojoLife people group to voice their interests, thoughts, and ideas.

Laying out a culture of open correspondence cultivates a feeling of solidarity and shared liability.

2. Laying out a Complaint Goal Cycle:

Execute an unmistakable complaint goal interaction to address clashes or worries inside the local area. This interaction ought to be fair, unprejudiced, and zeroed in on finding arrangements as opposed to doling out fault. Giving an organized component to debate goals keeps a sound and agreeable local area.

3. Local area Gatherings and City centers:

Customary people group gatherings or official Q&A events set out open doors for aggregate conversation. These discussions can address explicit difficulties, assemble input on possible enhancements, and cultivate a feeling of local area contribution. Inclusivity is critical, it is heard and considered to guarantee that assorted viewpoints.

4. Proficient Intervention and Guiding Administrations:

For challenges that require a more nuanced approach, consider including proficient go-betweens or instructors. These prepared experts can work with valuable discussions, intercede questions, and give direction on settling issues inside the local area while advancing comprehension and sympathy.

5. Schooling on Moral Practices:

Proactively address difficulties connected with moral practices by stressing training. Offer studios, classes, or instructional courses that support the significance of moral lead, sportsmanship, and regard inside the combative techniques local area. Teaching professionals from the very beginning keeps issues from emerging.

6. Administration Preparing and Advancement:

Fortify authority inside the McDojoLife people group by putting resources into preparing and advancement programs. Pioneers, including educators and local area coordinators, can profit from studios that improve relational abilities, compromise strategies, and moral initiative standards.

7. Variety and Incorporation Drives:

Challenges connected with variety and incorporation can be tended to through designated drives. Advance variety inside positions of authority, celebrate social mindfulness occasions and effectively look for input from professionals with changed foundations. A different and comprehensive local area is stronger and more versatile.

8. Ordinary Criticism Studies:

Carry out customary criticism studies to measure the local area's fulfillment and distinguish regions for development. Mysterious overviews can support legitimate reactions, giving important experiences into explicit difficulties and expected arrangements. This information-driven approach empowers local area pioneers to make informed choices.

9. Cooperative Critical thinking:

Cultivate a cooperative way to deal with critical thinking inside the McDojoLife people group. Urge experts to cooperate in tending to difficulties, utilizing the aggregate insight and imagination of the local area. Cooperative critical thinking fabricates a feeling of pride and fellowship.

10. Transformation to Evolving Conditions:

Perceive that difficulties inside the local area might advance over the long haul. Remain versatile and receptive to evolving conditions, changing methodologies on a case-by-case basis. The capacity to adjust guarantees that the McDojoLife heritage stays strong even with new difficulties.

11. Mentorship and Companion Backing Projects:

Lay out mentorship and friend support projects to reinforce associations inside the local area. Experienced specialists can act as tutors to newbies, giving direction and backing. Peer networks give a feeling of having a place and empower people to explore difficulties with the assistance of their combative techniques peers.

12. Festivity of Accomplishments and Achievements:

Balance difficulties by praising accomplishments and achievements inside the McDojoLife people group. Perceive and feature individual and aggregate triumphs, building up a positive and inspiring air. Recognizing progress cultivates inspiration and strength despite challenges.

By tending to difficulties inside the McDojoLife people group with a vital and cooperative methodology, professionals and pioneers can maintain the inheritance's obligation to persistent improvement, honesty, and the quest for greatness. The aggregate strength of the local area lies in its actual procedures as well as in its capacity to confront difficulties with solidarity, versatility, and a common obligation to the standards of combative techniques.

CONCLUSION

McDojoLife, a web-based stage, and local area, has turned into a huge voice in the combative techniques world, underlining the conservation of validness and customary preparation standards. Its experiences and heritage can be summed up as follows:

1. Uncovering McDojo Practices:

McDojoLife acquired conspicuousness for its job in uncovering what it considers McDojo rehearses — problematic and marketed approaches inside hand-to-hand fighting schools. By revealing insight into these practices, it intends to safeguard the trustworthiness of combative techniques.

2. Supporting for Realness:

McDojoLife

The tradition of McDojoLife lies in its obligation to advance legitimate combative techniques preparation. It urges specialists to look for schools and educators that focus on certifiable expertise improvement, regard for custom, and an emphasis on pragmatic self-protection.

3. Local area Mindfulness:

McDojoLife has constructed a local area where combative techniques devotees share encounters and experiences. By encouraging mindfulness and conversation, it enables people to make informed decisions while choosing a combative techniques school, advancing a local area-driven way to deal with hand to hand fighting training.

4. Social Regard:

The stage frequently stresses the significance of the social and verifiable underlying foundations of combative techniques. It urges professionals to embrace the upsides of discipline, lowliness, and regard that are

McDojoLife

indispensable to numerous conventional combative techniques.

5. Basic Assessment of Belt Frameworks:

McDojoLife has featured issues connected with belt advancements and testing, pushing for a more thorough and merit-based approach. This inheritance urges experts to assess the importance and genuineness of belt positions inside combative techniques schools.

6. Online People group Effect:

McDojoLife's inheritance stretches out past its web-based presence. Through web-based entertainment and different stages, it has impacted a change in hand-to-hand fighting in the local area, provoking conversations on quality guidance, moral practices, and the embodiment of combative techniques as a comprehensive discipline.

McDojoLife's heritage lies in its devotion to saving the legitimacy of combative techniques by uncovering and studying McDojo rehearses. It energizes a local area-driven, informed way to deal with hand-to-hand fighting schooling and stresses the significance of custom, social regard, and veritable expertise improvement inside the combative techniques local area. The eventual fate of bona fide combative techniques in the tradition of McDojoLife holds a few promising turns of events and difficulties. Here is an investigation of what lies ahead:

1. Expanded Mindfulness and Insight:

The McDojoLife inheritance has contributed fundamentally to bringing issues to light about the significance of knowing genuine combative techniques from McDojo rehearses. As this mindfulness keeps on developing, forthcoming hand-to-hand fighting understudies are probably going to turn out to be additional insightful buyers, searching out schools that focus on real preparation standards.

2. Accentuation on Instruction and Straightforwardness:

The tradition of McDojoLife empowers a culture of schooling and straightforwardness inside the hand-to-hand fighting local area. Real schools might view themselves as progressively constrained and straightforward about their genealogy, preparing techniques, and confirmation cycles to acquire and keep up with the trust of understudies.

3. Local area Driven Change:

The people group-driven nature of the McDojoLife heritage is probably going to encourage positive changes inside the combative techniques scene. As specialists share their encounters and bits of knowledge, an aggregate push for validness might prompt additional responsible and deferential hand-to-hand fighting in the local area.

4. Development of Belt Frameworks:

The tradition of McDojoLife has ignited discussions about the authenticity of belt frameworks. Later on, there might be a reexamination of belt positions, with a shift towards merit-based advancements and a reestablished accentuation on the worth and importance behind each position.

5. Reconciliation of Innovation:

With the rising job of innovation in training and correspondence, valid combative techniques schools might use online stages to give assets, associate with understudies, and offer information. This could upgrade availability to quality guidance while keeping up with the trustworthiness of customary preparation standards.

6. Worldwide Impact:

The McDojoLife heritage, being an internet-based stage with a worldwide reach, is probably going to keep impacting hand-to-hand fighting networks around the world. This worldwide point of view might add to the trading of thoughts, methods, and best works, advancing the combative techniques experienced by specialists all over the place.

7. Challenges in Commercialization:

Despite these positive patterns, difficulties might emerge in battling the commercialization of combative techniques. As the interest for validity builds, a few schools might endeavor to showcase themselves as veritable without proving their cases. Cautiousness and basic assessment will stay fundamental.

The eventual fate of true combative techniques in the McDojoLife heritage holds the commitment of a more educated, responsible, and deferential hand-to-hand fighting local area. As experts keep on focusing on veritable preparation standards, the tradition of McDojoLife will probably add to positive changes, encouraging a worldwide climate where hand-to-hand fighting flourishes with credibility and uprightness.

Made in United States
North Haven, CT
12 December 2024

62239538R00055